Lights, Camera, Fraction!

This CGP book has been carefully crafted to help Year 4 pupils build up all the Fractions and Decimals skills they need.

It's packed with quick-fire 10-Minute Tests that become more challenging as pupils work through — helping them get used to answering even the toughest questions.

We've even included full answers to every question — plus a handy chart to check progress too!

What CGP is all about

Our sole aim here at CGP is to produce the highest quality books — carefully written, immaculately presented and dangerously close to being funny.

Then we work our socks off to get them out to you — at the cheapest possible prices.

Published by CGP

Editors: Samuel Mann, Sean McParland, Caley Simpson and Ben Train

With thanks to Sarah George and Gail Renaud for the proofreading.

With thanks to Jan Greenway for the copyright research.

ISBN: 978 1 78908 641 6

Clipart from Corel®
Printed by W&G Baird Ltd, Antrim.

Based on the classic CGP style created by Richard Parsons.

Text, design, layout and original illustrations © Coordination Group Publications Ltd. (CGP) 2020
All rights reserved.

Photocopying this book is not permitted, even if you have a CLA licence.
Extra copies are available from CGP with next day delivery • 0800 1712 712 • www.cgpbooks.co.uk

Contents

Test 1 2
Test 2 4
Test 3 6
Test 4 8
Test 5 10
Test 6 12
Test 7 14

Test 8 16
Test 9 18
Test 10 20
Test 11 22
Test 12 24
Answers 26
Progress Chart 30

How to Use this Book

- This book contains <u>12 tests</u>, all geared towards improving your fractions and decimals skills.

- Each test is out of <u>10 marks</u> and should take about <u>10 minutes</u> to complete.

- Each test starts with some <u>warm-up questions</u> to get you going and ends with a <u>problem-solving question</u>.

- The tests <u>increase in difficulty</u> as you go through the book.

- <u>Answers</u> and a <u>Progress Chart</u> can be found at the <u>back</u> of the book.

Test 1

Warm up

1. a) Circle the number that is $\frac{1}{2}$ of 10.

    2   4   5   8   20

    1 mark

    b) Circle the number that is $\frac{1}{4}$ of 16.

    2   3   4   8   12

    1 mark

2. Circle the shape that has $\frac{1}{2}$ shaded.

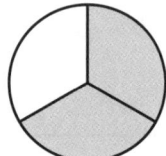  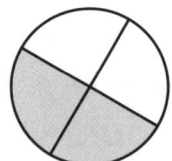 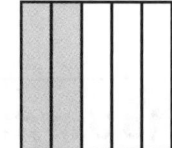

1 mark

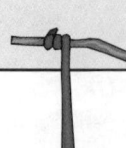
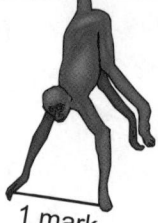

3. What fraction of the shapes below are circles?

  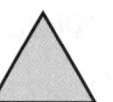

  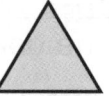

1 mark

4. Write a fraction in the gap to make each sentence true.

   One has been done for you.

   10 is $\frac{1}{2}$ of 20   5 is .... of 15

   6 is .... of 24   2 is .... of 16

   2 marks

5. Shade in one fifth of each shape below.

   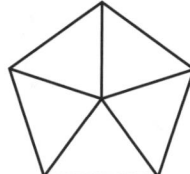 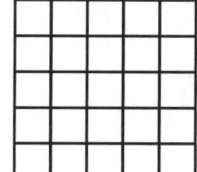 

   2 marks

6. A zoo has 40 animals.

   $\frac{1}{10}$ of the animals are hippos.

   $\frac{1}{4}$ of the animals are monkeys.

   How many hippos and monkeys are there in total?

   ....
   2 marks

END OF TEST

/ 10

Test 2

Warm up

1. What fraction of the crabs below are shaded?

....
1 mark

2. Count down in tenths from $\frac{8}{10}$.

$\frac{8}{10}$ .... $\frac{6}{10}$ ....

1 mark

3. Calculate the following:

$\frac{1}{2}$ of 16 = ... $\frac{1}{4}$ of 12 = ...

$\frac{1}{3}$ of 18 = ... $\frac{3}{4}$ of 20 = ...

2 marks

4. Work out:

$\frac{2}{7} + \frac{4}{7}$ = ... $\frac{8}{9} - \frac{3}{9}$ = ...

$\frac{3}{8} + \frac{2}{8}$ = ... $\frac{5}{6} - \frac{4}{6}$ = ...

2 marks

5. Write < or > in the box to make each number sentence true.

$\frac{1}{3}$ ☐ $\frac{1}{4}$ $\frac{1}{8}$ ☐ $\frac{1}{12}$

$\frac{2}{5}$ ☐ $\frac{4}{5}$ $\frac{7}{9}$ ☐ $\frac{4}{9}$

2 marks

6. Ella has 25 hats.

$\frac{3}{5}$ of her hats are bobble hats.

7 of her hats are sun hats.
The rest of her hats are fancy dress hats.

How many fancy dress hats does she have?

.... fancy dress hats

2 marks

END OF TEST

/ 10

Test 3

⏱ 10

Warm up

1. Tick the shapes that have $\frac{3}{8}$ shaded.

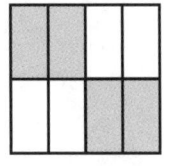 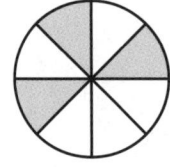 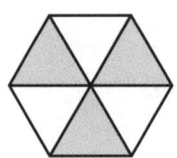 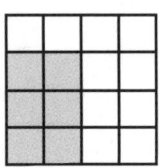 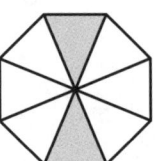

2 marks

2. Work out:

   a) $\frac{6}{7} - \frac{4}{7} =$ ....

   b) $\frac{3}{20} + \frac{14}{20} =$ ....

   c) $\frac{7}{15} + \frac{4}{15} =$ ....

   d) $\frac{10}{13} - \frac{6}{13} =$ ....

2 marks

3. Put these fractions in order, starting with the smallest.

   $\frac{1}{5}$ $\frac{1}{4}$ $\frac{1}{12}$ $\frac{1}{20}$

   ....

   1 mark

4. Shade the shape below to show an equivalent fraction.

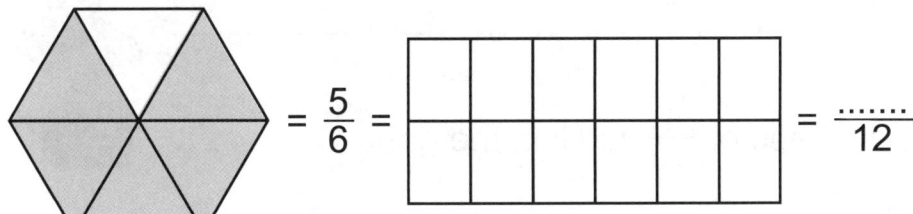 = $\frac{5}{6}$ = = $\frac{\ldots}{12}$

2 marks

5. Work out:

$\frac{11}{12} + \frac{8}{12}$ = ... $\frac{19}{11} - \frac{9}{11}$ = ...

1 mark

6. Vivek has a postcard collection.

$\frac{1}{3}$ of his postcards are from the USA.
He has 8 postcards from the USA.

$\frac{1}{2}$ of his postcards are from Europe.

How many postcards from Europe does he have?

.... postcards

2 marks

END OF TEST

/ 10

Test 4

Warm up

1. Count up in steps of $\frac{1}{10}$ to fill in the gaps.

   $\frac{2}{10}$ ....

   1 mark

2. Fill in the missing numbers to make these statements true.

   a) $\frac{7}{10} = \frac{\ldots}{100}$ b) $\frac{\ldots}{10} = \frac{90}{100}$

   1 mark

3. Look at this number line.

   What fractions are the arrows pointing to?

   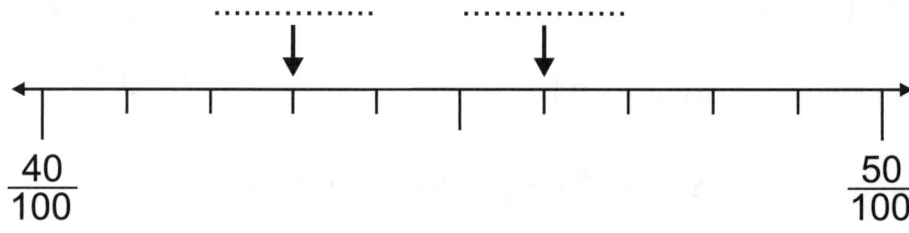

   2 marks

4. Work out:

   $\frac{5}{7} + \ldots = \frac{9}{7}$ $\frac{17}{6} - \ldots = \frac{12}{6}$

   $\frac{8}{9} + \frac{8}{9} = \ldots$ $\ldots - \frac{10}{12} = \frac{7}{12}$

   2 marks

5. Shade the second and third shapes so they have the same fraction shaded as the first shape.

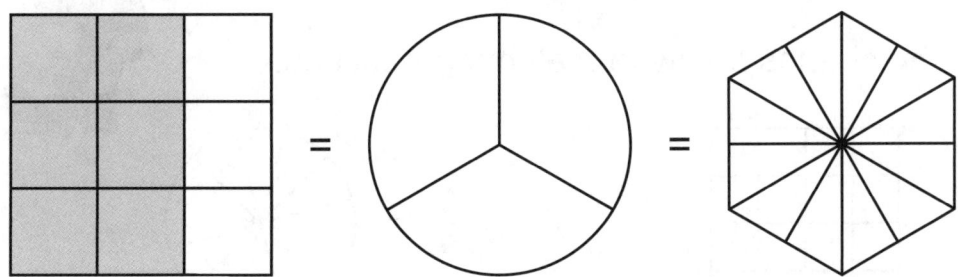

2 marks

6. A train has two carriages. There are 30 people in the first carriage. $\frac{1}{6}$ of them are getting off at the next stop.

There are 28 people in the second carriage. $\frac{3}{7}$ of them are getting off at the next stop.

How many people are getting off the train at the next stop?

.... people

2 marks

END OF TEST

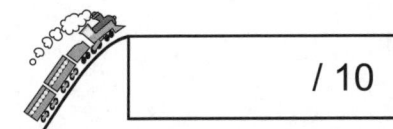

/ 10

Test 5

Warm up

1. Shade the shapes below to match the fractions.

   a) $\frac{1}{4}$ =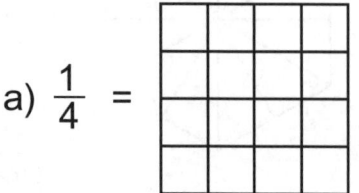

   b) $\frac{3}{4}$ =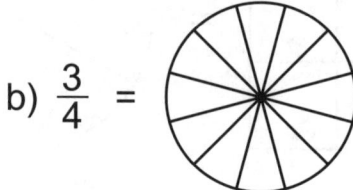

   2 marks

2. Circle the smaller fraction in each of these pairs.

   $\frac{1}{4}$ or $\frac{1}{8}$ $\frac{9}{12}$ or $\frac{11}{12}$ $\frac{4}{16}$ or $\frac{3}{16}$

   2 marks

3. Count in steps of $\frac{1}{100}$ to fill in the gaps below.

   .... $\frac{21}{100}$ .... $\frac{18}{100}$ ....

   1 mark

4. Write these fractions as decimals.

   $\frac{1}{2}$ = ... $\frac{3}{4}$ = ...

   1 mark

5. Fill in the gaps in these calculations.

$\frac{4}{5} + \ldots = \frac{12}{5}$ $\ldots - \frac{2}{8} = \frac{15}{8}$

$\ldots + \frac{13}{12} = \frac{20}{12}$ $\frac{27}{15} - \ldots = \frac{19}{15}$

2 marks

6. 56 children voted for the sport they wanted to play. They could choose either football, rugby or cricket. $\frac{2}{7}$ of the children voted for football. $\frac{3}{8}$ voted for rugby.

How many children voted for the most popular sport?

………… children

2 marks

END OF TEST

/ 10

Test 6

Warm up

1. Starting from $\frac{8}{100}$:

   a) count down 5 hundredths ....

   b) count up 3 hundredths ....

   2 marks

2. Fill in the gaps to split these numbers into ones, tenths and hundredths.

   a) 3.48 = ... + 0.4 + ...

   b) 7.19 = 7 + ... + ...

   2 marks

3. Draw lines to match each of these fractions to its equivalent decimal.

   One has been done for you.

   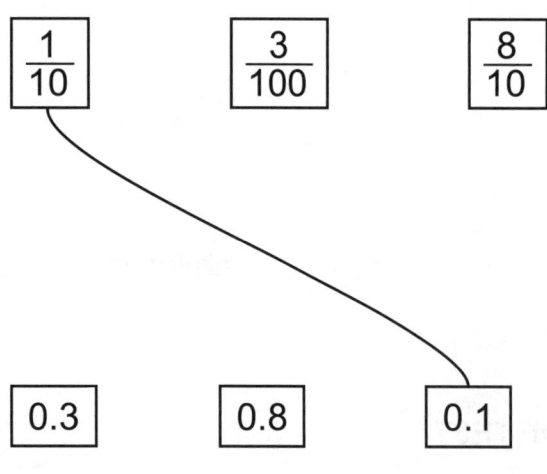

   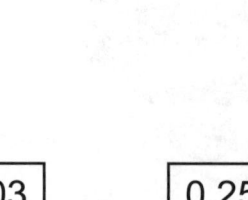

   2 marks

4. Work out the answers to these calculations as decimals.

5 ÷ 10 = ...   4 ÷ 100 = ...

19 ÷ 10 = ...   60 ÷ 100 = ...

2 marks

5. The prices of items at a corner shop are shown below.

Newspaper £0.75
Multipack of crisps £3.00
Ready meal £2.00

Jordan gets a discount on a ready meal, so he only has to pay $\frac{3}{4}$ of the normal price.

How much does Jordan save in pounds?

£ ....

1 mark

Eilis and nine of her friends split the cost of the most expensive item between them equally.

How much does Eilis spend in pence?

.... p

1 mark

END OF TEST

/ 10

Test 7

Warm up

1. Circle $\frac{2}{3}$ of the ducklings below.

                                                                             1 mark

2. Work out:

    a) $\frac{4}{5}$ of 10 = ...   b) $\frac{3}{4}$ of 16 = ...

    c) $\frac{9}{10}$ of 30 = ...   d) $\frac{5}{8}$ of 24 = ...

                                                                             2 marks

3. A grid is split into 100 equal squares. $\frac{71}{100}$ of the grid is shaded.

    How many more squares need to be shaded so that $\frac{83}{100}$ of the grid is shaded?

                                        .... squares   1 mark

4. Write these fractions as decimals.

    $\frac{9}{10}$ = ... $\frac{2}{10}$ = ...

    $\frac{7}{100}$ = ... $\frac{27}{100}$ = ...

                                                                             2 marks

5. Shade the diagram to help you find an equivalent fraction to the fraction below.

$\frac{21}{30}$ = 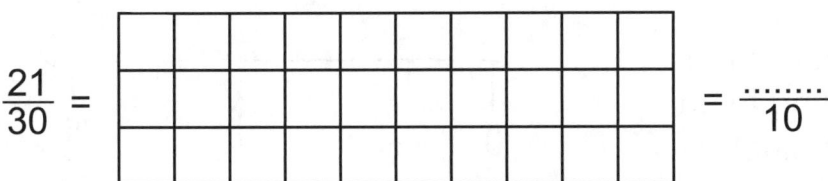 = $\frac{\ldots}{10}$

2 marks

6. A carton contains 2 litres of apple juice.

Isaac drinks $\frac{1}{4}$ of a litre of the apple juice.
Jessica drinks 0.2 litres of the apple juice.

How much apple juice is left in the carton?

Give your answer in litres, as a decimal.

.... litres

2 marks

END OF TEST

/ 10

Test 8

Warm up

1. What fraction is the arrow pointing to on this number line?

   .... 1 mark

2. Put these fractions in order, starting with the largest.

   $\frac{1}{8}$ $\frac{1}{25}$ $\frac{1}{6}$ $\frac{1}{10}$

   ....   1 mark

3. Complete the fractions below.

   $\frac{.....}{10} = 0.3$ $\frac{.....}{100} = 0.81$

   $\frac{7}{.....} = 0.07$ $\frac{.....}{100} = 0.4$

   2 marks

4. Circle the larger decimal in each pair.

   0.2 or 0.4   0.51 or 0.15   0.36 or 0.38

   2 marks

5. Write 10 or 100 in the gaps to make these calculations correct.

2 ÷ .... = 0.2   68 ÷ .... = 0.68

5 ÷ .... = 0.05   37 ÷ .... = 3.7

2 marks

6. Mrs Morris is taking her son to a museum.
Some prices for the museum are shown in the table below.

Adult ticket	£13.50
Child ticket	£6.25
Museum map	£2.40

Mrs Morris has £20. She wants to buy one adult ticket, one child ticket and one museum map.

How much more money does she need?

£ ....

2 marks

END OF TEST

/ 10

Test 9

Warm up

1. Fill in the gaps to make these calculations correct.

   a) 0.05 + ... = 1.15   b) .... + 0.7 = 2.73

   1 mark

2. Work out the answers to these calculations as decimals.

   a) 6 ÷ 10 = ...   b) 62 ÷ 100 = ...

   c) 3 ÷ 100 = ...   d) 18 ÷ 100 = ...

   2 marks

3. Circle all the fractions that are equivalent to $\frac{1}{3}$.

   $\frac{3}{9}$ $\frac{30}{100}$ $\frac{9}{21}$ $\frac{6}{18}$

   2 marks

4. Round each decimal to the nearest whole number.

   7.8 → ....   8.3 → ....

   3.1 → ....   4.5 → ....

   2 marks

5. Fill in the gaps to complete these calculations.

.... ÷ 10 = $\frac{7}{10}$ $\frac{3}{10}$ ÷ .... = $\frac{3}{100}$

1 mark

6. Rahul needs to buy some wooden planks to repair a chest of drawers.

Type of wood	Weight of one plank
Pine	3.7 kg
Oak	4.95 kg
Teak	4.89 kg

He buys one each of the heaviest and the lightest planks.

How much do the planks he buys weigh in total?

.... kg

2 marks

END OF TEST

/ 10

Test 10

Warm up

1. Circle all the decimals that are smaller than 5.34.

   5.28   5.43   5.35

   5.36   5.32

   1 mark

2. Round each decimal to the nearest whole number.

   a) 6.2 → ....   b) 2.7 → ....

   c) 1.8 → ....   d) 9.4 → ....

   2 marks

3. Draw lines to match each fraction to its equivalent decimal.

   | $\frac{7}{10}$ | $\frac{73}{100}$ | $\frac{7}{100}$ | $\frac{77}{100}$ |

   | 0.07 | 0.77 | 0.7 | 0.73 |

   2 marks

4. Fill in the missing numbers to make these calculations correct.

$\frac{9}{16} + \frac{\ldots}{16} = \frac{19}{16}$

$\frac{\ldots}{11} - \frac{9}{11} = \frac{8}{11}$

1 mark

5. Work out:

2.4 + 0.3 = ...

8.9 − 0.6 = ...

1.32 + 0.53 = ...

3.78 − 0.14 = ...

2 marks

6. Matt has 8 m of ribbon. He uses $\frac{1}{4}$ of the ribbon on a dress and 1.65 m of the ribbon on a skirt.

How much ribbon does he have left?

.... m

2 marks

END OF TEST

/ 10

Test 10

Test 11

Warm up

1. Write each fraction below as a decimal.

   a) $\dfrac{5}{100}$ = ...   b) $\dfrac{90}{100}$ = ...

   1 mark

2. Fill in the missing values to make equivalent fractions.

   a) $\dfrac{2}{3} = \dfrac{........}{15}$ b) $\dfrac{3}{8} = \dfrac{6}{........}$

   c) $\dfrac{........}{5} = \dfrac{20}{25}$ d) $\dfrac{3}{........} = \dfrac{18}{24}$

   2 marks

3. Circle **all** the decimals that round to 12 when rounded to the nearest whole number.

   11.5   12.8   12.4   11.7   11.4   12.5

   2 marks

4. Put a tick in the box next to the calculation that is correct.

   6.23 + 0.62 = 6.49   ☐

   6.23 + 0.62 = 6.85   ☐

   6.23 + 0.62 = 12.43   ☐

   1 mark

5. Write down the digit that will be in the tenths place of the answers to these divisions.

   7 ÷ 10   .... will be in the tenths place

   3 ÷ 100   .... will be in the tenths place

   38 ÷ 10   .... will be in the tenths place

   46 ÷ 100   .... will be in the tenths place

   2 marks

6. A shop has a special offer. If you buy two of the same item, the second one is half the price of the first.

Picture frame	£5.00
Candle	£2.00
Microscope	£12.40

   Meera buys two picture frames, two candles and a microscope.

   How much does she spend in total?

   £ ....

   2 marks

   END OF TEST

   / 10

Test 12

Warm up

1. Draw lines to match each calculation with its answer.

   | 3 ÷ 100 | | 33 ÷ 10 | | 33 ÷ 100 |

   3.3   0.03   0.33

   1 mark

2. Work out: a) $\frac{11}{17} + \frac{12}{17} = $ .... b) $\frac{32}{30} - \frac{13}{30} = $ ....

   1 mark

3. Madison scores eight out of ten in a spelling test.

   What is her score as a decimal?

   ....

   1 mark

   She scores ninety six out of one hundred in a maths test.

   What is her score as a decimal?

   ....

   1 mark

4. Fill in the missing numbers to make these calculations correct.

   5.3 + ... = 5.9   7.68 − .... = 7.45

   10.2 − .... = 9.6   4.87 + ... = 4.95

   2 marks

Test 12   24   © CGP — not to be photocopied

5. Draw lines to match each decimal in the top row to the nearest whole number in the bottom row.

| 97.5 | 95.8 | 94.3 | 95.1 | 96.9 |

| 94 | 95 | 96 | 97 | 98 |

2 marks

6. Camille and Justin both make cookies for a bake sale.

Camille uses 1 kg of white choc chips and 1.12 kg of milk choc chips.

Justin uses $\frac{3}{4}$ of the amount of white choc chips and twice the amount of milk choc chips as Camille.

How many kilograms of choc chips does Justin use in total to make his cookies?

.... kg

2 marks

END OF TEST

/ 10

Answers

Test 1 – pages 2-3

1. a) 5 (**1 mark**)   b) 4 (**1 mark**)
2. 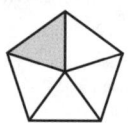 should be circled. (**1 mark**)
3. $\frac{4}{9}$ (**1 mark**)
4. 5 is $\frac{1}{3}$ of 15   6 is $\frac{1}{4}$ of 24   2 is $\frac{1}{8}$ of 16
    (**2 marks for all three correct, otherwise 1 mark for two correct**)
5. E.g.

    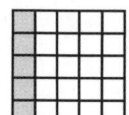 

    (**2 marks for all three shapes with correct amount shaded, otherwise 1 mark for any two correct**)
6. $\frac{1}{10}$ of 40 = 40 ÷ 10 = 4 hippos
    $\frac{1}{4}$ of 40 = 40 ÷ 4 = 10 monkeys
    So there are 4 + 10 = 14 hippos and monkeys in total.
    (**2 marks for the correct answer, otherwise 1 mark for a correct method**)

Test 2 – pages 4-5

1. $\frac{5}{7}$ (**1 mark**)
2. $\frac{8}{10}$ $\frac{7}{10}$ $\frac{6}{10}$ $\frac{5}{10}$ $\frac{4}{10}$ (**1 mark**)
3. $\frac{1}{2}$ of 16 = 8 $\frac{1}{4}$ of 12 = 3
    $\frac{1}{3}$ of 18 = 6 $\frac{3}{4}$ of 20 = 15
    (**2 marks for all four correct, otherwise 1 mark for at least two correct**)
4. $\frac{2}{7} + \frac{4}{7} = \frac{6}{7}$ $\frac{8}{9} - \frac{3}{9} = \frac{5}{9}$
    $\frac{3}{8} + \frac{2}{8} = \frac{5}{8}$ $\frac{5}{6} - \frac{4}{6} = \frac{1}{6}$
    (**2 marks for all four correct, otherwise 1 mark for at least two correct**)

5. $\frac{1}{3} > \frac{1}{4}$ $\frac{1}{8} > \frac{1}{12}$
    $\frac{2}{5} < \frac{4}{5}$ $\frac{7}{9} > \frac{4}{9}$
    (**2 marks for all four correct, otherwise 1 mark for at least two correct**)
6. $\frac{1}{5}$ of 25 = 25 ÷ 5 = 5, so $\frac{3}{5}$ of 25 = 5 × 3 = 15.
    So Ella has 25 – 15 – 7 = 3 fancy dress hats.
    (**2 marks for the correct answer, otherwise 1 mark for a correct method**)

Test 3 – pages 6-7

1.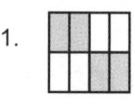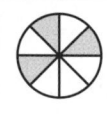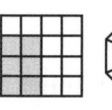
    ☐ ✓ ☐ ✓ ☐
    (**1 mark for each correct shape ticked, with no incorrect shapes ticked**)
2. a) $\frac{2}{7}$ b) $\frac{17}{20}$ c) $\frac{11}{15}$ d) $\frac{4}{13}$
    (**2 marks for all four correct, otherwise 1 mark for at least two correct**)
3. $\frac{1}{20}$ $\frac{1}{12}$ $\frac{1}{5}$ $\frac{1}{4}$ (**1 mark**)
4. $= \frac{5}{6} =$ 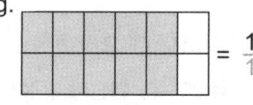 $= \frac{10}{12}$ E.g.

    (**1 mark for correct shading, 1 mark for correct numerator**)
5. $\frac{11}{12} + \frac{8}{12} = \frac{19}{12}$ $\frac{19}{11} - \frac{9}{11} = \frac{10}{11}$
    (**1 mark for both correct**)
6. 8 is $\frac{1}{3}$ of the total amount, so Vivek has 8 × 3 = 24 postcards. $\frac{1}{2}$ of 24 is 24 ÷ 2 = 12, so Vivek has 12 postcards from Europe.
    (**2 marks for the correct answer, otherwise 1 mark for a correct method**)

Answers

Test 4 – pages 8-9

1. $\frac{2}{10}$ $\frac{3}{10}$ $\frac{4}{10}$ $\frac{5}{10}$ $\frac{6}{10}$ (1 mark)
2. a) 70   b) 9
   (1 mark for both correct)
3.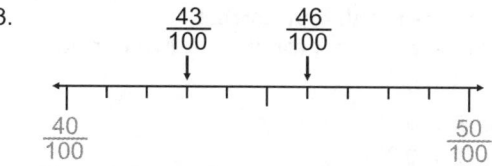
   (1 mark for each correct fraction)
4. $\frac{5}{7} + \frac{4}{7} = \frac{9}{7}$ $\frac{17}{6} - \frac{5}{6} = \frac{12}{6}$
   $\frac{8}{9} + \frac{8}{9} = \frac{16}{9}$ $\frac{17}{12} - \frac{10}{12} = \frac{7}{12}$
   (2 marks for all four correct, otherwise 1 mark for at least two correct)
5. E.g.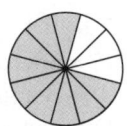
   (1 mark for each shape with the correct amount shaded)
6. $\frac{1}{6}$ of 30 is 30 ÷ 6 = 5, so 5 people are getting off the first carriage. $\frac{1}{7}$ of 28 is 28 ÷ 7 = 4, so $\frac{3}{7}$ of 28 is 4 × 3 = 12. So 12 people are getting off the second carriage.
   So 5 + 12 = 17 people are getting off the train.
   (2 marks for the correct answer, otherwise 1 mark for a correct method)

Test 5 – pages 10-11

1. a) E.g.   b) E.g.
   (1 mark for each shape with the correct amount shaded)
2. $\frac{1}{8}$, $\frac{9}{12}$ and $\frac{3}{16}$ should be circled.
   (2 marks for all three correct fractions circled, otherwise 1 mark for two correct fractions circled)
3. $\frac{22}{100}$ $\frac{21}{100}$ $\frac{20}{100}$ $\frac{19}{100}$ $\frac{18}{100}$ $\frac{17}{100}$
   (1 mark)
4. $\frac{1}{2}$ = 0.5 $\frac{3}{4}$ = 0.75
   (1 mark for both correct)
5. $\frac{4}{5} + \frac{8}{5} = \frac{12}{5}$ $\frac{17}{8} - \frac{2}{8} = \frac{15}{8}$
   $\frac{7}{12} + \frac{13}{12} = \frac{20}{12}$ $\frac{27}{15} - \frac{8}{15} = \frac{19}{15}$
   (2 marks for all four correct, otherwise 1 mark for at least two correct)
6. $\frac{1}{7}$ of 56 is 56 ÷ 7 = 8, so $\frac{2}{7}$ of 56 is 8 × 2 = 16.
   So 16 children voted for football.
   $\frac{1}{8}$ of 56 is 56 ÷ 8 = 7, so $\frac{3}{8}$ of 56 is 7 × 3 = 21.
   So 21 children voted for rugby.
   So 56 – 16 – 21 = 19 children voted for cricket.
   Rugby has the most votes, so 21 children voted for the most popular sport.
   (2 marks for the correct answer, otherwise 1 mark for a correct method)

Test 6 – pages 12-13

1. a) $\frac{3}{100}$ (1 mark)   b) $\frac{11}{100}$ (1 mark)
2. a) 3.48 = 3 + 0.4 + 0.08
   b) 7.19 = 7 + 0.1 + 0.09
   (1 mark for each correct calculation)
3.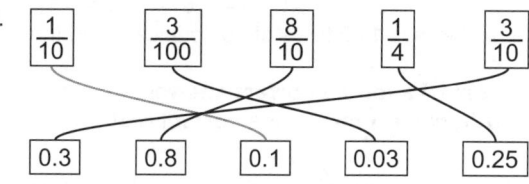
   (2 marks for all four lines correct, otherwise 1 mark for at least two correct)
4. 5 ÷ 10 = 0.5   4 ÷ 100 = 0.04
   19 ÷ 10 = 1.9   60 ÷ 100 = 0.6
   (2 marks for all four correct, otherwise 1 mark for at least two correct)
5. The normal price of a ready meal is £2.00.
   $\frac{3}{4}$ of £2.00 is £1.50, so he saves
   £2.00 – £1.50 = £0.50. (1 mark)

   The most expensive item is the multipack of crisps, which costs £3.00.
   They split the cost between the ten of them, so divide the cost by 10: £3.00 ÷ 10 = £0.30.
   So Eilis spends £0.30, which is 30p. (1 mark)

Test 7 – pages 14-15

1. E.g.

   (**1 mark for the correct number of ducklings circled**)

2. a) 8   b) 12   c) 27   d) 15
   (**2 marks for all four correct, otherwise 1 mark for at least two correct**)

3. $\frac{83}{100} - \frac{71}{100} = \frac{12}{100}$, so 12 more squares need to be shaded. (**1 mark**)

4. $\frac{9}{10} = 0.9$ $\frac{2}{10} = 0.2$
   $\frac{7}{100} = 0.07$ $\frac{27}{100} = 0.27$
   (**2 marks for all four correct, otherwise 1 mark for at least two correct**)

5.

   (**1 mark for the correct number of squares shaded, 1 mark for the correct numerator**)

6. $\frac{1}{4} = 0.25$, so Isaac and Jessica drank 0.25 litres + 0.2 litres = 0.45 litres in total. 2 − 0.45 = 2 − 0.4 − 0.05 = 1.6 − 0.05 = 1.55, so there is 1.55 litres of apple juice left in the carton.
   (**2 marks for the correct answer, otherwise 1 mark for a correct method**)

Test 8 – pages 16-17

1. $\frac{3}{10}$ (**1 mark**)

2. $\frac{1}{6}, \frac{1}{8}, \frac{1}{10}, \frac{1}{25}$ (**1 mark**)

3. $\frac{3}{10} = 0.3$ $\frac{81}{100} = 0.81$
   $\frac{7}{100} = 0.07$ $\frac{40}{100} = 0.4$
   (**2 marks for all four correct, otherwise 1 mark for at least two correct**)

4. 0.4, 0.51 and 0.38 should be circled.
   (**2 marks for all three correct, otherwise 1 mark for two correct**)

5. 2 ÷ 10 = 0.2   68 ÷ 100 = 0.68
   5 ÷ 100 = 0.05   37 ÷ 10 = 3.7
   (**2 marks for all four correct, otherwise 1 mark for at least two correct**)

6. ```
     1 3.5 0
       6.2 5
   +   2.4 0
   ─────────
     2 2.1 5
         1 1
   ```
   The tickets and map cost £22.15 in total, so she needs £22.15 − £20 = £2.15 more.
   (**2 marks for the correct answer, otherwise 1 mark for a correct method**)

Test 9 – pages 18-19

1. a) 0.05 + 1.1 = 1.15   b) 2.03 + 0.7 = 2.73
   (**1 mark for both correct**)

2. a) 0.6   b) 0.62   c) 0.03   d) 0.18
   (**2 marks for all four correct, otherwise 1 mark for at least two correct**)

3. $\frac{3}{9} = \frac{1}{3}$, $\frac{30}{100} = \frac{3}{10}$, $\frac{9}{21} = \frac{3}{7}$, $\frac{6}{18} = \frac{1}{3}$
   So $\frac{3}{9}$ and $\frac{6}{18}$ should be circled.
   (**1 mark for each correct fraction circled**)

4. 8   8
   3   5
   (**2 marks for all four correct, otherwise 1 mark for at least two correct**)

5. 7 ÷ 10 = $\frac{7}{10}$ $\frac{3}{10}$ ÷ 10 = $\frac{3}{100}$
   (**1 mark for both correct answers**)

6. 4.95 > 4.89 > 3.7, so oak planks are the heaviest and pine planks are the lightest.
   ```
     4.9 5
   + 3.7 0
   ───────
     8.6 5
     1
   ```
   So the planks he buys weigh 8.65 kg in total.
   (**2 marks for the correct answer, otherwise 1 mark for a correct method**)

Answers
   ```

Test 10 – pages 20-21

1. 5.28 and 5.32 should be circled.
   (**1 mark for both correct**)
2. a) 6   b) 3   c) 2   d) 9
   (**2 marks for all four correct,
   otherwise 1 mark for at least two correct**)
3.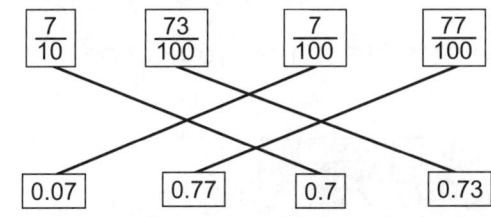
   (**2 marks for all four lines drawn correctly,
   otherwise 1 mark for two correct lines**)
4. $\frac{9}{16} + \frac{10}{16} = \frac{19}{16}$ $\frac{17}{11} - \frac{9}{11} = \frac{8}{11}$
   (**1 mark for both correct**)
5. 2.4 + 0.3 = 2.7   8.9 – 0.6 = 8.3
   1.32 + 0.53 = 1.85   3.78 – 0.14 = 3.64
   (**2 marks for all four correct,
   otherwise 1 mark for at least two correct**)
6. $\frac{1}{4}$ of 8 m = 8 ÷ 4 = 2 m.
   So Matt has 8 – 2 – 1.65 = 6 – 1.65 = 4.35 m of ribbon left.
   (**2 marks for the correct answer,
   otherwise 1 mark for a correct method**)

Test 11 – pages 22-23

1. a) 0.05   b) 0.9
   (**1 mark for both correct**)
2. a) $\frac{2}{3} = \frac{10}{15}$ b) $\frac{3}{8} = \frac{6}{16}$
   c) $\frac{4}{5} = \frac{20}{25}$ d) $\frac{3}{4} = \frac{18}{24}$
   (**2 marks for all four correct,
   otherwise 1 mark for at least two correct**)
3. 11.5, 12.4 and 11.7 should be circled.
   (**2 marks for the correct three decimals
   circled and no others, otherwise 1 mark for
   one or two correct decimals circled and no
   more than one other decimal circled**)
4. 6.23 + 0.62 = 6.85 ☑   (**1 mark**)

5. 7 will be in the tenths place
   0 will be in the tenths place
   8 will be in the tenths place
   4 will be in the tenths place
   (**2 marks for all four correct,
   otherwise 1 mark for at least two correct**)
6. $\frac{1}{2}$ of £5.00 = £2.50, so two picture
   frames cost £5.00 + £2.50 = £7.50.
   $\frac{1}{2}$ of £2.00 = £1.00, so two candles
   cost £2.00 + £1.00 = £3.00.
   So in total Meera spends
   £7.50 + £3.00 + £12.40 = £22.90.
   (**2 marks for the correct answer,
   otherwise 1 mark for a correct method**)

Test 12 – pages 24-25

1.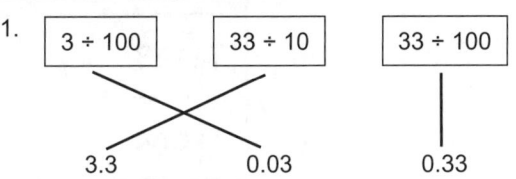
   (**1 mark for all three lines correct**)
2. a) $\frac{23}{17}$ b) $\frac{19}{30}$
   (**1 mark for both correct**)
3. Eight out of ten = $\frac{8}{10}$ = 0.8 (**1 mark**)
   Ninety six out of one hundred = $\frac{96}{100}$
   = 0.96 (**1 mark**)
4. 5.3 + 0.6 = 5.9   7.68 – 0.23 = 7.45
   10.2 – 0.6 = 9.6   4.87 + 0.08 = 4.95
   (**2 marks for all four correct,
   otherwise 1 mark for at least two correct**)
5.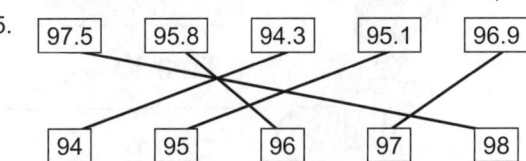
   (**2 marks for all five lines drawn correctly,
   otherwise 1 mark for three correct lines**)
6. Justin uses $\frac{3}{4}$ of 1 kg = 0.75 kg of white
   choc chips and 1.12 kg × 2 = 2.24 kg of milk
   choc chips. So in total he uses
   0.75 kg + 2.24 kg = 2.99 kg of chocolate chips.
   (**2 marks for the correct answer,
   otherwise 1 mark for a correct method**)

Progress Chart

That's all the tests in the book done — nice one!

Now fill in this table with all of your scores and see how you got on.

	Score
Test 1	
Test 2	
Test 3	
Test 4	
Test 5	
Test 6	
Test 7	
Test 8	
Test 9	
Test 10	
Test 11	
Test 12	